WHAT TASKS CAN COMPUTERS PERFORM?

BOBI MARTIN

Britannica®
Educational Publishing

IN ASSOCIATION WITH

ROSEN
EDUCATIONAL SERVICES

Published in 2018 by Britannica Educational Publishing (a trademark of Encyclopædia Britannica, Inc.) in association with The Rosen Publishing Group, Inc.
29 East 21st Street, New York, NY 10010

Distributed exclusively by Rosen Publishing.
To see additional Britannica Educational Publishing titles, go to rosenpublishing.com.

First Edition

Britannica Educational Publishing
J.E. Luebering: Executive Director, Core Editorial
Mary Rose McCudden: Editor, Britannica Student Encyclopedia

Rosen Publishing
Bernadette Davis: Editor
Nelson Sá: Art Director
Nicole Russo-Duca: Series Designer
Cindy Reiman: Photography Manager
Sherri Jackson: Photo Researcher

Library of Congress Cataloging-in-Publication Data

Names: Martin, Bobi, author.
Title: What tasks can computers perform? / Bobi Martin.
Description: New York : Britannica Educational Publishing, in Association with Rosen Educational Services, 2018 | Series: Let's find out! : computer science | Includes bibliographical references and index. | Audience: Grades 1-4.
Identifiers: LCCN 2017018664| ISBN 9781680488579 (library bound) | ISBN 9781680488562 (pbk.) | ISBN 9781538300374 (6 pack)
Subjects: LCSH: Microcomputers—Juvenile literature. | Internet—Juvenile literature.
Classification: LCC QA76.52 .M376 2017 | DDC 004.16—dc23
LC record available at https://lccn.loc.gov/2017018664

Manufactured in the United States of America

Photo credits: Cover and back cover maxsattana/iStock/Thinkstock; p. 4 librakv/Shutterstock.com; p. 5 © iStockphoto.com/Alacatr; p. 6 Kekyalyaynen/Shutterstock.com; p. 7 Guido Mieth/Taxi/Getty Images; p. 8 Hadrian/Shutterstock.com; p. 9 © iStockphoto.com/EH Stock; p. 10 © iStockphoto.com/Anatolii Babii; p. 11 © iStockphoto.com/Photojournalis; p. 12 Bloomicon/Shutterstock.com; p. 13 PA Images/Alamy Stock Photo; p. 14 Wavebreakmedia/Shutterstock.com; p. 15 Justin Sullivan/Getty Images; p. 16 GongTo/Shutterstock.com; pp. 17, 22 NASA; p. 18 Wdnet Studio/Alamy Stock Photo; p. 19 Antonio M. Rosario/The Image Bank/Getty Images; p. 20 PC Gamer Magazine/Future/Getty Images; p. 21 Arterra/Universal Images Group/Getty Images; p. 23 © NASA Jet Propulsion Laboratory; p. 24 Westend61 GmbH/Alamy Stock Photo; p. 25 Rawpixel.com/Shutterstock.com; p. 26 Neirfy/Shutterstock.com; p. 27 Barcroft/Barcroft Media/Getty Images; p. 28 Kyodo News/Getty Images; p. 29 Film Factory/Shutterstock.com; interior pages background © iStockphoto.com/pinglabel.

CONTENTS

Computers Are Amazing

A computer is a device that works with and displays information. The information can be words, pictures, movies, or sounds.

Computer information is called data. Computers process data very quickly. Because they work quickly, they can finish tasks faster than people can. They make fewer errors, too.

Computers come in many forms and can perform many tasks. Supercomputers are very powerful. They do complex tasks like tracking

Laptops, tablets, and cell phones are all computers. People use them for different purposes.

These servers are housed together in a large room called a server room. They have to be kept cool so they won't overheat.

▶▶

THINK ABOUT IT

Computers help people do things faster and easier. How would people's lives be different without computers?

the weather. Servers are powerful computers that just store information. Desktop personal computers, or PCs, are used in offices, at school, and at home. People use these computers to send email, write reports, shop, do their banking, listen to music, and play games. Laptops and tablet computers do the same things as PCs, but they are smaller and easier to carry. No matter what size they are, computers are amazing.

THE COMPUTER'S BODY

A computer system has both hardware and software. Hardware is the physical parts of the computer, or the parts you can touch. Software is made up of the programs, or sets of instructions, that the hardware stores and processes.

All computers have the same hardware. Computers keep data, including software and files, on a storage device called a hard drive. Hardware that accesses software and files to make it available to the

Computer hardware includes things such as a keyboard, a mouse, and a monitor. They work together to complete tasks.

Computer apps are software that allow the user to perform tasks on a computer.

microprocessor is called random-access memory (RAM). The microprocessor is the computer's brain. It is also called the central processing unit (CPU).

Software is divided into two basic types—the operating system (OS) and application software (app). The OS controls how different parts of the hardware work together. Apps tell the computer how to do specific tasks like word processing or playing games.

COMPARE AND CONTRAST

Why do you think the CPU is called the computer's brain? Compare and contrast the kinds of tasks a human brain and a CPU do.

THE OPERATING SYSTEM

The operating system (OS) is the software that runs a computer. Without it, a computer's other software could not perform any tasks. The OS directs the **input** and output of data, manages a computer's memory, and keeps track of files. It also includes maintenance software, called utility software.

An OS communicates with other attached devices, such as a keyboard, as well as with internal hardware.

Install critical update

A critical update is available and you should install it as soon as possible.

You won't be able to use your phone while the update installs. This should take 5 to 10 minutes, but could take longer.

Windows Phone 8.1 (8.10.14219.341) - This update can help make your phone work even better.
Lumia Update for Windows Phone.

Updating software is one of the tasks an operating system performs. Updates help keep the computer healthy.

VOCABULARY

Input is information that is entered into a computer.

When a person types on a keyboard, the OS directs the CPU to process the information that the person typed. When the CPU has processed the information, the data appears where it belongs on the screen.

Early computers could only do one task at a time. Today's computers can perform many tasks at the same time. Operating systems help this happen.

Microsoft Windows and Mac OS are two operating systems for desktop computers. Android and iOS are examples of operating systems for tablets and smartphones.

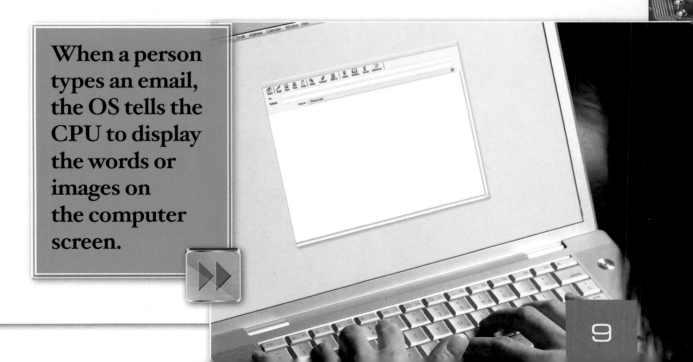

When a person types an email, the OS tells the CPU to display the words or images on the computer screen.

APPLICATION SOFTWARE

Application software are also known as computer programs. Programs that run on tablets or smartphones are often simply called apps. Programs give a computer instructions for doing specific tasks that the user wants to complete. These tasks may include sending email or making video calls.

Some programs just do one or two things. And some types of apps function differently on a PC than they do on other computer devices.

These apps connect to social media. They are able to access the internet without using a browser.

Music apps store sound files and let people choose what songs they want to hear. They also recommend music.

For example, clock programs on PCs mostly just display the time. However, clock apps on smartphones and tablets can also be set to wake someone at a certain time or to let the user know about an appointment.

COMPARE AND CONTRAST

Compare and contrast the way apps work on PCs, tablets, and smartphones.

Many programs can also help a computer perform multiple tasks. Photo apps let people edit their photos, save them, share them with others, and print them. Music apps let a user download music or play it. The best apps work well and take up little space.

TEACHING COMPUTERS NEW TASKS

PCs, tablets, and smartphones always come with some programs preinstalled, or installed in advance. People can teach their computers to do new tasks by downloading and installing new apps. Many of them are even free! They can also uninstall, or delete, apps that they no longer need or to make space for other apps.

Users can add apps to their smartphone or tablet from an app store or from other places.

Some apps add new features to software already on the computer. These are called add-ons. For example, a grammar app can check spelling and punctuation on a

Security and utility programs scan files on a computer to look for viruses. Users can also download and install utility programs.

Virus and Spyware Protection

Checking status.

Firewall Protection

Checking status.

McAfee Web Protection

Checking status.

Threats Detection

Checking status.

Checking status.

word processor or some other text program. Add-ons can also hide or take away unwanted features, like advertisements.

Security programs help protect computers from **viruses** or other software that can harm the computer. Antivirus software can spot viruses and delete them before they damage a computer or its files.

VOCABULARY

Viruses are harmful software that damage or destroy data and try to spread themselves.

UNDERSTANDING THE INTERNET AND THE WEB

The internet is a network, or system, that connects millions of computers worldwide. The internet allows people to connect to each other and to share

information. People access that information through the World Wide Web, or the web. Users search for information on the web through a program called a browser. Browsers like Chrome, Safari, and Firefox locate many web pages or sites that might have the right information.

Some schools allow their students and workers to access the local intranet but not the wider internet.

A web browser can help users access almost any website, including social networks.

Some businesses, including many schools, share information using an intranet. Like the internet, an intranet is a computer network. The difference is that an intranet is a private network, so it can only be used by people who work within that company or school.

THINK ABOUT IT

Browsing involves looking at many things to see if there is something interesting. Do you think the name "browser" fits this software? Why or why not?

15

The web has millions of websites. A website typically consists of several web pages, or individual files and associated media. People create websites using a language called hypertext markup language, or HTML. Browsers read HTML and allow people to view websites on the computer. Each website has its own internet address, called a uniform resource locator, or URL. Many URLs begin with "www," which stands for "World Wide Web." Search engines like Google or Yahoo allow browsers to search for specific information on websites.

The internet can be accessed from almost anywhere, even from a space station high above Earth.

But there is more to the internet than browsing. People also use the internet to send emails, play games, buy and sell products, play movies and music, and share videos and photos.

COMPARE AND CONTRAST

How are the internet and the web the same? How are they different?

READING, WRITING, AND MORE!

Many people use computers to help with tasks at home and school, such as writing reports and keeping track of data. Word processing programs allow users to create all kinds of written documents. A user can type the information, format it so that it looks the way the user wants, and then save the file to the computer. The user can open the file later and make changes and then print out the

Users can make a bar graph on their tablet or computer to help them track their spending or do calculations.

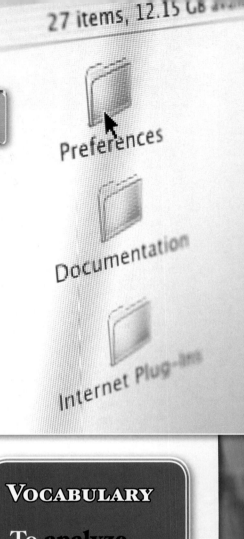

27 items, 12.15 GB a...

Preferences

Documentation

Internet Plug-ins

A computer's directory arranges data and programs in folders. Icons of the folders make the data easier to find.

document. The programs even have built-in dictionaries that check for spelling errors.

Spreadsheet programs are also popular. These programs allow users to store and **analyze** many different types of data. Spreadsheets also allow users to collect data and present it in an organized way and to manage it to provide further information. For example, spreadsheets can sort information, share it with other users, and create graphs, such as bar graphs and pie charts.

VOCABULARY

To **analyze** is to study and compare information.

EXPERIMENTING WITH COMPUTERS

Computers calculate large amounts of data. In fact, modern microprocessors can perform billions of math calculations per second!

Scientists often use computer simulations to find solutions to real problems. A simulation is a model of an event or situation. First, a scientist must input data into a computer program. The computer will then examine the data to calculate how a real-life system would act based on the

A computer's microprocessor (*center*) is powerful but tiny. It works with other tiny parts.

Scientists are not the only people who use simulations. Computer simulators are also used to teach people to do jobs, such as flying airplanes.

input. One simulation might try to find out at what temperature a plant can grow instead of actually trying to grow the plant. Engineers might use computers to design complicated machines such as spacecraft. Other scientists might then use a computer simulation to plan a mission to another planet for the spacecraft.

THINK ABOUT IT

Why might a scientist want to use a computer simulation rather than observing a real event?

Computers on the Move

Most robots are machines that are controlled by computers. An industrial robot is an arm-like machine that can turn at several joints. It has hand-like parts to grasp and hold things. Computer software controls the movements of the robot and tells the hardware what to do. Some industrial robots move and load materials. Others help build things on assembly lines, such as cars. Some doctors use robots, too. Robots help surgeons

Some robots are made to look, move, and talk like people.

perform operations that were not possible before. The surgeon controls the robot from a computer near the operating table.

Robots are also used in space to go where people cannot survive. The Mars Exploration Rovers were robotic vehicles that explored the surface of Mars. The robots had cameras and instruments for examining rocks, soil, and dust. Cameras on the rovers let scientists see what the rovers saw. The rovers sent data back to the scientists through computers.

COMPARE AND CONTRAST

Compare and contrast the ways doctors, scientists, and factories use computers.

The Mars Exploration Rovers examined rocks, soil, and dust. They then sent data on those samples back to scientists on Earth.

23

DISPLAYING INFORMATION

Computers display different kinds of information through output devices. This data can be fixed images, text, videos, or audio.

Input devices can capture data that can be shared later. A web camera, or webcam, and a microphone can capture sound and video. Using a keyboard can create text. And special devices can capture drawings.

The text, photos, drawings, and videos are displayed on the computer monitor. The text and images

This photographer is examining and editing photographs.

Graphic designers use interactive software and a special pad to draw images displayed on a computer screen.

can be sent to an output device called a printer. Speakers allow a user to hear audio files.

Hardware displays or captures data, but software lets users **interact** with the data. Art software lets people create images, or

graphics. A computer's graphical user interface (GUI) is one means through which users communicate with a computer. Icons, or small linked images, appear on the screen. A user can point to an icon using a mouse and click on it to open programs or files.

GAMERS!

Video games are software that require user input in order to advance the game's events. Players control the action of a game by using a controller. Video games keep people entertained, but they may also be used to train or teach someone a set of skills.

A user can download game apps from the web or buy them in a store. When choosing a game, the user should make sure it is compatible with the computer or console that will run it.

After a game is installed, the computer's microprocessor can run the program. The program's instructions control sounds and the graphics that

Users play games on their smartphones, but computers or consoles are more powerful.

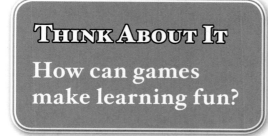

THINK ABOUT IT

How can games make learning fun?

appear on the screen. The instructions also evaluate whether the player is winning or losing.

Some games only allow one person to play at a time. Some older games allow up to four players. Online gaming lets people team up with or compete against massive numbers of video game players across the internet.

After an illness, this young girl learned to walk again by using balance games on a Wii Fit board.

WHAT WOULD WE DO WITHOUT THEM?

New types of computerized devices and new uses for devices are created every year. Some businesses use drones, or small flying robots, to deliver packages. Computers on the ground control the drones by telling them where to go and what to do. Drones were even programmed to put on a flying light show at the 2017 Super Bowl.

This drone in Chiba, Japan, is being tested for delivery. Drones come in many shapes and sizes.

Smartphones let people access or send data from almost anywhere. They are the most mobile device.

Smartphones let us shop online, play games, and send email and text messages. Smartphones and computers in cars display maps to help people find places. They warn people if their car needs its oil changed or when there is not enough air in the tires.

People use computers in some way every day. What would we do without them?

THINK ABOUT IT

Computers are changing the way people work and play. What kinds of changes do you think computers will bring in the future?

GLOSSARY

browser A computer program that provides access to information on a network and especially to websites.

download To copy a file to a computer's storage device from the web or from a different storage device.

drone A small flying robot that is controlled by a computer.

email A system for sending and receiving digital messages.

file A collection of data considered as a unit.

hard drive A device for storing computer data that consists of one or more hard disks in a sealed case.

hardware The physical parts of a computer.

hyperlink A link that allows users to move quickly from one place in a document to another place in the same or different document or website.

laptop A small personal computer with a screen, keyboard, and built-in mouse or touchpad that can be carried.

search engine A software program that looks for specific information on websites.

smartphone A cell phone with a touch screen that can connect to the internet.

tablet A small, flat computer that receives input by touch rather than through a keyboard and mouse.

text message A message that may contain text, images, videos, and attachments that is sent to a phone number. It is sent through cell phone towers instead of over the internet.

For More Information

Books

Coleman, Miriam. *Designing Computer Programs* (Software Engineers). New York, NY: PowerKids Press, 2016.

Diehn, Andi. *Technology: Cool Women Who Code* (Girls in Science). White River Junction, VT: Nomad Press, 2015.

Faust, Daniel. *Building Computers* (Computer Engineers). New York, NY: PowerKids Press, 2016.

Masura, Shauna. *Digital Badges* (21st Century Skills Innovation Library: Makers as Innovators). Ann Arbor, MI: Cherry Lake Publishing, 2014.

Taylor-Butler, Christine. *Computers* (A True Book). New York, NY: Children's Press, 2017.

Websites

Because of the changing nature of internet links, Rosen Publishing has developed an online list of websites related to the subject of this book. This site is updated regularly. Please use this link to access this list:

http://www.rosenlinks.com/LFO/Tasks

INDEX